365

STYLE AND FASHION TIPS FOR WOMEN

Claudia Piras and
Bernhard Roetzel

The authors:
Claudia Piras is an author and freelance journalist writing for various lifestyle magazines. In addition to her interest in culinary matters, she also specializes in the fields of fashion and living trends. Bernhard Roetzel is a freelance fashion journalist and contributes regularly to established magazines such as "Men's Health" and "Manager Magazine," as well as numerous other specialist publications. He has already published several books on fashion.

The tips contained in this book have been carefully compiled and checked by the authors, editors and publishers. No guarantee can be given, however, nor can any liability be accepted on the part of the authors, editors, publishers or their representatives for personal injury, damage to property or financial loss.

Cover illustrations: JOOP! GmbH, Hamburg (www.joop.com), Hugo Boss AG, Metzingen (www.hugoboss.com), Montblanc Deutschland GmbH, Hamburg (www.montblanc.com)

Original edition
© 2002 DuMont monte Verlag, Cologne
   (DuMont monte UK, London)

Author: Claudia Piras and Bernhard Roetzel
Production: Königsblau, Nicole Gehlen
Translation: Susan Ghanouni in association with First Edition Translations Ltd
Editing: David Price in association with First Edition Translations Ltd
Typesetting: First Edition Translations Ltd, Cambridge, UK
Overall production: Mladinska, Slowenien

ISBN 3-8320-7108-3
Printed in Slovenia

Contents

THE PERFECT BUSINESS LOOK

Being appropriately dressed for business is important – and can even be a factor in determining your career. It is therefore a good idea to take an objective look at yourself from time to time and consider what sort of image you and your clothes are projecting. Does it reflect your capabilities and your position? Does it conform to your company's dress code? Remember: First impressions count!

1

Your business clothes should make you look as professional as possible, no matter how young you are. Avoid anything that makes you look cute as this may make people reluctant to take you seriously. Have confidence in yourself – you do not need to resort to cheap tactics to win people over.

Blazers or jackets that have a center vent at the back or side vents should not be too tight-fitting, otherwise they will gape unattractively. This will have an unflattering effect on even the most perfectly proportioned bottom!

3

Do not wear a tie with a pantsuit (trouser suit), however popular this look may be in fashion magazines. This style is too affectedly masculine for the business world.

Do you have an early meeting first thing in the morning, followed by a full day at the trade fair, and finally, dinner in a restaurant with an important client? Make sure you leave those new shoes at home in the wardrobe! If you have a marathon session like this, it is wiser to rely on comfortable old favorites, in which you will stand a realistic chance of making it through the day.

4

Treat yourself to a good quality clothes brush with natural bristles – and use it! Regular brushing gets rid of any dust or dirt from your clothes, as well as unattractive dandruff, fluff, or hair.

5

6

When buying clothes, keep an eye out for garments with tasteful buttons made from natural materials like horn, mother-of-pearl, or corozo. Nasty plastic imitations can spoil an outfit. If a particular garment really appeals to you, apart from its buttons, and it fits well, you can always invest in a set of new, better-quality buttons.

7

You will only feel confident and self-assured if you are wearing clothes you like and in which you feel comfortable. Never choose clothes that make you feel too "dressed up" for important meetings or occasions.

8

Business clothes should be clean and immaculately kept. Do not put stained or worn outfits back in the wardrobe, but send them straight to the cleaners so that they are ready next time they are needed.

9

No matter how plain or strict your company's dress code may be, make sure you steer clear of outfits that make you look like a governess or maiden aunt, and avoid garments with big bows at the neck, blouses with stand-up collars, and clumpy shoes. Otherwise you risk unwittingly creating a comical parody of the sober business look.

Blazers, pantsuits and suits should be pressed professionally. If you do decide to take matters into your own hands, always use a linen or cotton ironing cloth to prevent getting shiny patches on the material.

10

11

If you are standing and are engaged in a long conversation, it is perfectly acceptable to put your hands in your pockets or cross your arms from time to time so as to vary your position a little. You should, however, never have your left hand in your pocket when shaking someone's hand in greeting or in farewell.

A good sense of style means avoiding the latest fashion gimmicks, which are likely to be *passé* by tomorrow anyway.

12

13

Pinstripes are still a classic business look, suitable for either men or women. A more conservative and elegant effect is produced when the pinstripes are discreet and widely spaced, rather than thick stripes close together, which can look rather vulgar and contrived.

14

If you have found a designer you like, then stick to that designer. Mixing lots of different labels can easily make you seem like a fashion victim and may imply a lack of confidence.

15

If you are attending a function where you are likely to meet a lot of people, it is a good idea to have a number of visiting cards to hand. If you would rather not be rummaging about in your briefcase or purse (handbag) every time, you could keep the cards in your jacket pocket. Remember not to leave any leftover cards in your pocket, however, but get rid of them at the end of the day. Crumpled, dog-eared cards make a very bad impression.

You will know when a blazer is a good fit, in other words not too tight and not too loose, if you can do up the buttons easily and at the same time be aware that it is fastened.

16

17

If you frequently find yourself having to carry files or other business material around with you, then invest in a lady's briefcase and steer clear of overly large, bulky, or predominantly masculine-looking bags. Heavy attaché cases look anything but stylish on women.

Although blazers and suit jackets are equipped with pockets, they are not intended to be filled to the brim. It is better to leave them empty so that they do not bulge unattractively, adding extra inches to your hips.

18

Jangling earrings and ethnic bracelets may lend a certain eccentric look to your appearance, but are too noisy for an office environment. In an atmosphere where quiet concentration is called for, your colleagues might find such jewelry very irritating.

19

20

A dark, single-breasted blazer is the ultimate business classic. It can be worn with straight, charcoal-colored pants or, if you want a more casual look, with khaki pants or even jeans.

21

You accidentally knock over a glass during a meeting. Do not make a major drama out of it as it can happen to anyone. If anything has gone on your own outfit, mop the material with a handkerchief. If the liquid has landed on anyone else, make your apologies and, if necessary, offer to have the garment dry-cleaned.

22

The blouse under your business suit should not be taut, nor should it gape open, revealing your flesh and bra underneath. This does not look sexy, it just looks cheap. Make sure you try on any blouses or shirts before you buy them as a precautionary measure. If you have difficulty in finding standard sizes to fit you, perhaps you should consider treating yourself to some tailor-made garments.

If you have a long journey to work, it is perfectly acceptable to wear a warm and fleecy or padded jacket in winter, even though, stylistically speaking, this may not go so well with your sophisticated business outfit. No one should have to freeze in a thin coat, and it is not as if your client is going to see you in your cozy survival outfit.

23

Whatever hemlines may be currently in fashion, it is far more important to wear the length of skirt that suits you and your figure. Petite women should be particularly cautious when it comes to below-the-knee or calf-length skirts as these can easily make them look even smaller.

24

25

A light-colored top emphasizes the upper body, while light-colored trousers draw attention to the legs. Which parts of your figure would you like to highlight?

26

No matter how bad an itch you may have, or how irritating something may feel, scratching of any kind on any part of your body is absolutely taboo in the presence of others.

27

The flimsy wire hangers that you get from the dry-cleaners wreak havoc with the sensitive shoulders of dresses and jackets. Hang them as quickly as possible on thick, wooden or plastic hangers that are appropriately shaped.

28

Do not experiment with clothes for an important meeting. It is better to rely on tried and tested outfits that you have worn in similar situations and which you know make you feel well-dressed, comfortable and self-confident.

Gray basics need not be boring, particularly if they are livened up with a few strong colors. Gray looks good with red, burgundy, all shades of violet, blue, black, dark green, pink – in fact, any color you want.

29

Buy yourself a large, three-sided mirror with adjustable wings, in which you can see yourself from all sides and from behind. You can then make certain that your outfit is perfect all the way round.

30

You may have at least ten suits hanging in the wardrobe, but none of them fits properly. Do not be tempted to buy another ready-made, but seek out a good tailor who can make you one to measure. This will prove a worthwhile investment, for this kind of outfit is a timeless classic.

31

32

Has your figure undergone any changes? If you have put on or lost weight after the birth of a child or an illness, do not immediately get rid of any clothes that have become too tight or too big. Be patient and wait and see how your weight settles down before making any decisions.

Pantsuits and skirt suits are equally acceptable for businesswear. You are not obliged, therefore, to wear a skirt if you do not wish to.

33

34

Take a realistic look at your company's dress code and make a mental note of what your colleagues are wearing. Your own outfit should not make you appear under- or overdressed.

If you like wearing a white blouse, try to avoid applying makeup to your neck. Makeup marks on the collar look anything but attractive.

35

36

Scarves are a good way of livening up a business outfit. Colors and patterns can be varied. Nevertheless, accessories should remain just that and not become the main item of your outfit.
The important thing is not to opt for scarves or wraps that are too big, or else they will look too voluminous and dominate the rest of your outfit.

Bringing home too many purchases at a time means that the individual garments do not get enough appreciation or attention. There is nothing sadder than immediately confining new acquisitions to the wardrobe – your new treasures deserve a better fate.

37

38

Treat yourself to some really fashionable shoes to complement your classic suit or pantsuit. In this way, even the most timeless of styles or materials will still look like the height of fashion.

39

If you wish you could wear the same outfit every day, for instance your unbeatable pantsuit, then do so – if you feel comfortable in it. Make this uniform of yours your particular trademark.

Even very conservative companies (such as banks, insurance companies, law companies) now accept women wearing trousers, with the exception, of course, of tight jeans, Bermuda shorts or other casual attire.

40

41

Black and white form a rather harsh contrast. A more elegant and subtle color combination would be to combine black with cream or light beige. Alternatively, you could substitute black for a dark charcoal gray.

42

Business clothes are not cheap and, accordingly, need to be chosen with care. Find a clothes store where you can expect professional advice and are allowed plenty of time to try on the garments. Do not let yourself be rushed. You are under no obligation to buy if you do not want to, no matter how much time the sales assistant has devoted to you.

Keep your business wardrobe as simple as possible – and make sure that the different items coordinate well with each other.

43

44

Perfect clothes are no substitute for personality, good manners, and charm.

45

If you have the opportunity, buy a pair of trousers which matches the new skirt suit, or, conversely, buy a skirt that would go with the jacket of the new pantsuit. In this way, you can vary your outfit.

Rolled-up sleeves were a popular
fashion statement in the 1980s, but
now look hopelessly outmoded.
If your sleeves are too long, have
them shortened.

46

If you cannot decide between a patterned or a self-colored
material, go for the self color. This will make it easier for you to
find suitable accessories.

47

48

Make sure that your handbag and shoes match. If you are wearing a belt, this, too, must fit into the color scheme. Black shoes need a black handbag, whereas brown tones offer more flexibility. Even dark reds or greens go well with brown.

49

When you are buying blouses and shirts, check that the collar feels comfortable. If it does not sit properly, or irritates or impedes movement in any way, you will never really feel happy with the garment, no matter how expensive it is.

Invest in a good quality, camelhair coat. It will go with nearly all your business outfits and will also prove useful for your out-of-work activities.

50

51

52

Your opposite number will associate a simply defined outfit with a clear, straightforward, competent personality. Leave all superfluous ornamentation aside and you will automatically show yourself in your best light. If you want to add a special touch that underlines your personality, do so by way of a particular accessory.

Shoes with high, stiletto heels look very elegant for business – provided that they are well cared for and in an excellent state of repair. Wrinkled or scuffed leather, resulting from the shoe getting caught between paving stones, in drains or air vents, will ruin your whole appearance.

Soft leather gloves are a popular accessory in cold weather. If you shake somebody's hand in the street, it is fine for you to leave your gloves on, but indoors, you should remove your gloves before shaking anybody's hand.

53

54

Do you wish you had slimmer hips? Have the pockets removed from your trousers and the side seams sewn up. If you want to make your stomach look flatter, choose trousers zipped at the side, preferably without front pleats.

The type and weight of material should reflect the current season. A cozy tweed jacket will look as out of place in summer as a lightweight linen suit would at a Christmas party.

55

56

If you work in a somewhat conservative environment, it would perhaps be better not to wear your long hair loose. Tie it back into a pony tail or wear it up. This will make you look more professional.

Buy the more expensive items of your wardrobe only in stores which do their own alterations on the premises and are equipped to make a professional job of altering your expensive blazer, valuable coat, or exclusive pantsuit.

57

58

If you notice a woman who is particularly well dressed, admire her – then set yourself the task of working out what it is that makes her look so good. What does her outfit consist of? What colors has she chosen? What sort of a figure has she got and how has she emphasized its good points? What is her makeup like? And so on. If you make this sort of analysis, be it from photos or real-life subjects, it will improve your natural instinct for good looks.

59

Empty belt loops are fine with jeans or khaki pants, but if you are wearing pants for work, you should use them for the purpose for which they were intended, by threading a good-quality belt through them. Alternatively, remove them (or have them removed by a professional seamstress).

60

Business outfits should be classy and timeless, but this does not mean that you have to go on wearing them forever. Retire long-serving skirt and pantsuits and treat yourself to a new ensemble.

CASUALWEAR FOR RELAXATION

Over the past ten years, leisure wear and sportswear have assumed an increasingly important role in the fashion stakes. Wearing fashionably stylish outfits in your free time and at weekends has become a mark of culture and lifestyle. Furthermore, casual clothes are becoming acceptable in an increasing number of situations and business environments. Reason enough, therefore, to get rid of the baggy sweatshirt and old jogging pants once and for all.

You may not be one of the tallest people in the world, but flat shoes, especially those of a high-quality make, look cool even on petite women and encourage a relaxed and easy style of walking.

61

Is your wardrobe bursting at the seams. Why not try a "clothes by season" system? Pack your heavy items away at the end of the winter. This will give you more space and a clearer view of your light-weight clothing. When the days begin to draw in again, pack all your summer things into a large suitcase and store it in the attic, under the bed, or in the basement. Make sure everything is clean when you pack it away – and don't forget the mothballs!

62

63

Do not make a point of wearing your old clothes during your free time – except perhaps for gardening or working on the car. Scruffy old clothes suggest a lack of self-respect. Treat yourself to nice clothes, even just for wearing at home – you owe it to yourself.

64

Wash new shirts, T-shirts, or other items to be worn next to the skin before wearing them for the first time. This will remove traces of chemicals left from the manufacturing process, and will guard against skin irritations.

65

Nothing ruins an outfit so much as self-doubt. Wear what you feel like wearing – and feel utterly confident about your appearance. Do not torment yourself wondering if the red polo shirt would have looked better with your beige trousers or whether classic loafers would have been better than modern designer sneakers. You are wearing the outfit now – and that should be an end to it!

66

Tight-fitting trousers are chic and sexy, but if you do not have ultra-slim thighs or calves, it is better to wear something slightly looser that will have a slimming and flattering effect on the figure.

Shoulder pads create an unnaturally square outline. They are certainly not needed in T-shirts or pullovers. Snip them out, throw them away, and hope they never come back into fashion.

67

68

Are you planning a complete change of style or just looking for ideas to make a few small changes? Visit a large clothes store and try on the sort of clothes you would otherwise never have contemplated wearing. You dislike dresses? Right then, take as many as you can carry into the changing-room. You hate trousers? Try some on. You might be surprised at what suits you and what you like.

Sleeveless tops make your bust look bigger. However, you need good, firm arms to look good in them. Hard, wrinkled skin around your elbows and loose flesh under your upper arm do not look attractive. Careful skin care and a regular keep-fit routine using weights can help in this case.

69

70

Suede is leather with a napped surface and should be maintained accordingly. Carefully brush in an upwards direction the pile of any shiny patches using a special eraser or wire brush.

71

Never overestimate your figure. Short miniskirts, cropped tops, hipster trousers all need a good figure to carry them off. If you do not have the figure of a fashion model, be independent and leave others to look ridiculous in such outfits.

If you suffer from hot flushes, wear a cardigan rather than a pullover and loose scarves instead of tight-fitting collars. In this way, you can always remove a layer before you start perspiring too much. Avoid tight-fitting T-shirts and bodies which cling to your figure.

72

A casual style of dress should be reflected in your hair and makeup. An elaborate hairstyle, false eyelashes, and dramatically red lipstick look out of place with jeans and a T-shirt.

73

74

If you are planning a shopping trip, be realistic. Do not try to buy five outfits in one go, complete with all the requisite accessories – three or four items are the absolute limit. Choosing these carefully will be quite taxing enough.

75

Never clothe yourself from head to foot in one single color. An outfit entirely in red, green, yellow, or blue will look too bold and lack subtlety, an all-gray outfit is boring, and an all-black one looks too funereal. A contrasting color accent, even if it is only a brightly colored brooch, is what is needed to set the outfit off.

Little animals, hearts, teddy bears, etc. are very cute, it's true, but not when adorning the clothes of a mature woman. The same applies to any other "cute" forms of ornamentation. They should be left well alone once you have outgrown your teenage years.

76

Vertical stripes give a figure height and are useful for the fuller figure as well as for more petite women. If you are tall to start with and do not want to appear even taller, however, steer clear of vertical stripes.

77

Deciding in advance what outfit to wear and not just throwing on items at random in the morning is obviously the sensible thing to do and should be part of our daily routine. Do not carry this to extremes, however, and allow fashion to become a source of stress. Most of the people you encounter during the course of a day will not notice what you are wearing in the first place, and even if they do, will quickly forget again. As a matter of interest, ask ten people if they remember what you were wearing the previous day. What will stick in people's minds is the overall impression you create: in other words which style category you fit into, whether feminine, casual, sexy, extravagant, natural, romantic, practical, inconspicuous, or whatever

78

79

Although quilted jackets are fashionable, they can be very voluminous. In order to avoid looking like the Michelin man, it is best to choose a slim-fitting style, preferably with raglan sleeves. If you are very petite, it might be best to ask yourself whether wearing a feather duvet really does do anything for you or you just end up looking like a little ball on legs.

If it is a casual look you are aiming for, then make sure you get it right. Leave anything connected with your classic business outfit to one side. Most fashion mistakes are the result of carelessly mixing elements from the two styles, for example, combining casual sneakers or soft casual shoes with a formal black handbag that you would use for the office.

80

81

Fashion is a process of change. However convinced you may feel at the moment that a particular look is exactly right for you and you will never want any other, you may well have changed your mind in a year's time and have a new favorite look.

82

Whichever sport you do in your free time, it is essential that you are equipped with suitable high-quality footwear. Not only will you look stylish, but the right footwear saves wear and tear on your tendons, ligaments, and joints.

Even at the height of summer, evenings can be quite cool. If you are invited to a garden party or some other open-air event, make sure you take a light jacket along with you. You do not necessarily need your dark winter cardigan; a lighter version with a high cotton content will look much brighter and fresher and still serve the purpose.

83

Black leather can be somewhat problematic. Unless you are a female rocker or the leather gear carries an outlandishly expensive designer label, it rarely achieves the right effect. Be wary about outfits consisting entirely of leather, such as leather skirts and jackets or pantsuits: You can easily have "too much of a good thing."

84

85

Women with fuller figures frequently try to hide their curves under unflattering, loose clothes. It is far better to go for clothes which are a good fit, regardless of size. Tent-like creations do not make you look thin, just shapeless.

86

Even casual clothes for leisure wear should be chosen and assembled with care. Do not be tempted by the pack of five unprepossessing T-shirts on special offer, but spend your money on one top with a good label which fits perfectly and really suits you. Quality should always take precedence over quantity.

87

Your clothes should be a source of pleasure to you. If you do not enjoy wearing a particular jacket, pair of trousers etc., then other people will not enjoy looking at you in them. Any clothes which you are unhappy about should be sent to the recycling bin!

88

Leisure clothes should reflect the lifestyle we lead, be fashionable, look comfortable and have a weekend feel-good air about them. Why do we not apply the same criteria to our business wardrobe? The right clothes need not automatically be stiff, conservative, old-fashioned, or uncomfortable.

89

Lacoste or Ralph Lauren polo shirts are suitable for almost any kind of casual wear and, in some companies, are even considered suitable for the office.

Even if you are dressing casually, shoes and trousers should still be in proportion to each other. Wide cargo trousers are best worn with sturdy sport shoes, even the heavy, chunky type. Narrow drainpipe jeans or summery capri trousers require daintier footwear, e.g. flat ballerina-style pumps.

90

91

Do not go overboard with your sportswear. An outdoor survival outfit designed to withstand Arctic temperatures will look silly if you just want to take the dog for a five-minute winter's walk round town. And if you are just cycling down the road, you do not need to be decked out with the full cyclist's kit of water flask, team shirt and special shoes. Simple leisure wear is much more appropriate.

92

Do not let anyone influence you in your choice of which clothes to buy. Even if the man in your life or your best friend thinks that a particular outfit looks fantastic on you, you yourself must ultimately be the one to decide whether you like yourself in it. It is your outfit, after all.

93

We often come to associate certain clothes with certain events. If you are sensitive to such sentiments, do discard any items that have unpleasant associations for you. Subconsciously, you no longer feel comfortable in them anyway, and are only making it unnecessarily difficult for yourself to leave the past behind and look positively toward the future.

94

Beware of colors that are all the rage at any given time (you will know which these are when they suddenly appear in every fashion magazine and store window.) By next season they will almost certainly look outdated.

95

Jogging suits are intended for jogging in, not for shopping at the supermarket or wandering around town at the weekend.

96

Sunglasses may look cool, but it is extremely
uncool (not to mention discourteous) to leave them
on indoors.

Wash dark-colored sweatshirts, shirts, and sweaters inside out to prevent them picking up light bits of fluff. If clothes do emerge from the washing-machine covered in fluff, there is only one solution: remove the fluff by careful brushing or by running a sticky roller over the individual garments. Fluff creates a very ill-groomed appearance.

97

98

If you are having difficulty deciding what really suits you, ask a friend to photograph, or, better still, video you in several different outfits. This will put you in a better position to assess your appearance more objectively.

99

Do not hang knitwear on hangers or it will lose its shape. Fold up any delicate knitted garments and reserve a suitably sized compartment for them in a cupboard or wardrobe.

Be true to your own particular style when choosing leisure wear. If you normally go around sporting a classic golf look, a hippy XXL shirt is going to look completely out of place in your wardrobe – and on you.

100

101

Have you finally found a make of T-shirts, tops, blouses and other basics that are made exactly the way you like them? In really attractive material and in precisely your kind of style? Congratulations! Stock up and buy yourself a whole stack of them.

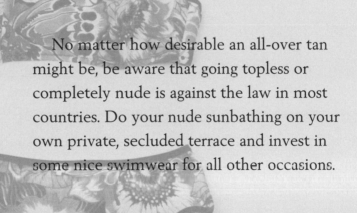

No matter how desirable an all-over tan might be, be aware that going topless or completely nude is against the law in most countries. Do your nude sunbathing on your own private, secluded terrace and invest in some nice swimwear for all other occasions.

102

103

If you are planning a shopping spree, a simple hairstyle is a must, especially if you going to be trying on sweaters, T-shirts, or sweatshirts. Once you have pulled three different garments over your head, you are bound to look pretty dishevelled. Another alternative is to take the clothes home with you and try them on in peace and quiet, without having to worry about your hair.

One more tip for your shopping trip: Wear a buttoned top, which you can take off and put on with minimal fuss. This will hopefully make you less reluctant to try things on, which you do need to do if you want to avoid buying the wrong thing.

104

SPECIAL OCCASIONS

Be it a gourmet dinner in an exclusive restaurant, a sophisticated ball or the gala première of your favorite opera, there are plenty of special occasions which warrant getting dressed up in your best evening wear. It is worthwhile taking a little extra trouble with your hair, makeup and outfit, as your efforts will underline the special nature of the occasion and augment the enjoyment.

If you are not used to wearing high-heeled shoes, you should spend a bit of time practicing before the big night. Tottering around unsteadily in unfamiliar shoes will detract from even the loveliest of outfits. If you are worried about not being able to last an entire evening in high heels, you would do better to choose shoes with lower heels.

105

106

If you are buying a dress with a very low-cut neckline, make sure that you can still move about in it confidently and easily.

107

What do the words "evening dress" mean on an invitation? For men, this means a dark formal suit, tuxedo or evening tailcoat, while women are expected to wear a long evening dress, and in winter, a long evening coat. If the hosts specifically request a particular dress code, it would be exceedingly impolite to ignore this request and turn up inappropriately dressed.

108

How do you react if someone spills cocktail sauce or red wine over your evening dress? Let them see what a classy lady you are by reacting with a sense of humor. Do what you can to remove the mark, but then try and put it out of your mind.

Two ladies turn up at the party, ball, or gala event wearing the same outfit. If yours is not one of the dresses in question, then act as if you had not noticed the unfortunate occurrence. If yours docs happen to be one of the duplicate outfits, then keep your cool and make contact with your "twin for the evening" (have yourselves photographed together etc.). If, for any reason, this proves impossible and the evening is spoiled for you, then make an early departure.

109

110

If you have decided to really get dressed up, then make sure you do it properly, paying attention to every detail. Wearing clogs with a little black number will look absolutely ridiculous. Get into those high-heeled shoes, even if they are not all that comfortable.

Although, in theory, a black skirt worn with a white blouse is a suitable outfit for an afternoon reception, it does tend to look rather like a waitress's outfit. The two garments must be of excellent quality. Never ever team them with a black waistcoat.

111

Turning up at an evening gathering wearing unsuitably casual or even scruffy clothes constitutes a serious breach of etiquette and is offensive, not only to the hosts, but also to the other guests. If you really have nothing whatsoever to wear, then you should either buy something suitable or decline the invitation in the first place.

113

If you are going to a special function, leave your spacious business purse at home. Evening bags are inevitably small and impractical – but a lipstick and handkerchief are all you need for such occasions anyway.

Invest in a timeless "little black dress." With this simple knee-length (or shorter), figure-hugging cocktail dress in your wardrobe, you will be equipped for almost any evening occasion.

114

Occasions which demand a long evening dress include balls and any event prefixed by the word "gala," such as gala premières, gala dinners, etc.

115

116

It is acceptable for women, unlike men, to keep wearing their hats or other headgear indoors.

It is difficult to color-coordinate shades of white and the result may look peculiar. If you are, however, determined to wear white with white, then try and match the shade of the garments as exactly as possible. There are more shades of white than you might think. The same is true of black.

117

118

There may well be no fixed rules any longer about what people should wear for the opera, operetta or theater, but it is still a special evening. Out of respect for the musicians, singers, dancers, or actors, you should refrain from turning up in normal everyday clothes and wear something smart instead.

If you are planning a special hairstyle for your big evening, it is best to try it out beforehand to see whether you can manage to create your coiffure masterpiece without help. If not, you will have to fit in an appointment at the hairdresser just before the event – or else choose a different hairstyle.

119

120

You can leave on your long evening gloves all through the glittering evening. You do not even need to remove them to shake hands.

121

Close-fitting long skirts should be made from stretch fabric or else have a slit at the bottom to save the wearer from having to totter about. No matter how exclusive and expensive your evening dress, you still have to be able to move about reasonably normally in it, otherwise your outfit is bound to look peculiar, if not downright ridiculous.

If you receive an invitation to a wedding, do feel free to enquire about the dress code and whether it is to be a big, traditional celebration or a more casual affair. What you must avoid at all costs is dressing in such a way as to outshine the bride. The bride is the leading lady of the day and nobody must steal the limelight from her!

122

Never buy a dress for a special occasion, for which you have to starve yourself before you can get into it. What happens if you cannot stick to your diet or your weight loss turns out to be less than planned? You will find yourself with no outfit to wear.

123

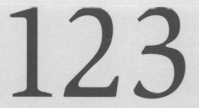

If you are going out in the evening to some special function, you should try and organize your schedule so that you can spend some time relaxing in the afternoon. You will feel more rested and relaxed than if you leave yourself no spare time and have to get ready at the last minute.

124

125

Many women feel nervous or self-conscious when they find themselves in unaccustomed, confusing, or intimidating situations and tend to fiddle with their hair, their earrings, the handle of their handbag, or anything else that comes to hand. Try and control this urge. It makes you look awkward and self-conscious.

126

Have you managed to obtain tickets for an opera première? Enjoy yourself – and remember: men should wear a dark suit or tuxedo and women, a cocktail dress or long evening dress. Hair should be coiffured, take extra care with your makeup and give your hands a fresh manicure. You owe it to the occasion.

127

Even a simple business pantsuit can be revamped into a glamorous, elegant evening outfit. Wear the jacket buttoned up over an invisible body, or open over a glittery top. Complete the effect with a stylish necklace or a long string of pearls, a diamanté patent leather evening bag and high-heeled shoes.

For those really special days or evenings that occasionally crop up, it is worth digging a little deeper into your pocket. Treat yourself to the luxury of having your makeup done professionally by a beautician or makeup artist. Book your appointment well in advance!

129   128

Be wary of using small evenings bags which have a magnetic fastening. These can play havoc with credit cards, or any other sort of plastic smart card, making them completely unreadable.

130

Who is escorting you to this important evening function and what will your partner be wearing? Couples look particularly striking when their two outfits are well coordinated in terms of style and color. This does not imply, however, that you must dress to match each other.

131

You are alone at a party, do not know a single soul and feel out on a limb. Take heart and simply approach someone. The correct way to introduce yourself in informal circles is to say: "Hello, I'm…" State your name clearly and do not mumble. A good way to break the ice is to mention straight away how you know the hosts. This gives the other person a topic of conversation he can latch onto. Try it – you'll see that it works.

132

How about, instead of going for a plunging neckline, opting for a low-cut back as a sexy and sophisticated alternative? This is also the perfect solution if the skin around your neck and chest area is no longer quite what it used to be.

If you are wearing a close-fitting evening dress, it is very important to have a perfect silhouette. If necessary, resort to undergarments that enhance your shape. Try these on beforehand, however, to make sure they still allow you adequate freedom of movement. A long evening at the opera wearing a corset that makes you look ten pounds lighter but scarcely allows you to breathe, will not be a very pleasant experience.

133

It would be regarded as a social gaffe to appear underdressed at a special function. However, it is equally wrong to be overdressed. Turning up for an informal or intimate get-together in overly elegant or formal attire is an affront to the other guests present.

134

Everyday shoes are not a suitable accompaniment to an evening dress. Treat yourself to a pair of elegant, but, ideally, neutral evening shoes. The shoes may be expensive, but the investment will be worthwhile. Since they will not be worn very frequently, they will last almost indefinitely.

136

Have your evening outfit dry-cleaned after wearing it for that special occasion and store it flat in a large chest. This is better than hanging it on a hanger. Do not forget the mothballs. You might wish to put a small sachet of potpourri in with it so that the garment smells pleasantly fresh next time you want to wear it.

137

It can become quite cool or draughty at evening functions, or you may want to step outside into the fresh air for a little while and take in enough oxygen to see you through the next ten dances. A stole that matches your dress, or a large neutral cashmere shawl would be perfect, both elegant and fashionable at the same time, and it will keep you warm.

LINGERIE AND ESSENTIALS

Lingerie, pantyhose (tights) and stockings are the most personal items of our wardrobe. Despite this, or perhaps for this very reason, they should not be overlooked. Wearing good lingerie is an ideal way of pampering yourself a little bit every day. We wear good lingerie first and foremost for our own pleasure and not to please others. Lingerie must be a perfect fit, on no account should it pinch or dig into your flesh – and it should reflect the personality of the wearer.

Treat yourself to some pretty lingerie which makes you feel wonderfully feminine. This will increase your positive self-esteem, you will stand taller and you will immediately look and feel more attractive and self-assured.

138

139

European women like to show off their bare legs. There is of course nothing wrong with this, at least out of working hours. Take care, though, in the USA, where pantyhose or stockings are *de rigueur* (even in high summer). This is especially true of the business world.

Materials made of modern micro-fibers are ideal for underwear: Light, elegant, sporty, breathable and, unlike cotton, they retain their shape.

140

141

If you plan to wear tight-fitting trousers or skirts, but want to avoid what Woody Allen called the "VPL" (visible panty line), buy yourself some G-strings or thongs.

Silk is not elastic and will not mould itself to your body shape. It is not an ideal material for bras and panties, therefore, but perfect for camisoles or negligées. Being such a delicate fabric, silk requires special care and should be washed at a low temperature, using a detergent designed for delicate fabrics.

142

143

Black lingerie can be too harsh a contrast with pale skin. An elegant midnight blue may be better, as this color is flattering to any skin type. Classic dark gray is another flattering alternative.

144

Is your butt too flat or shapeless? There are special panties available on the market which can provide a little padding or support to this part of the body.

145

Do you always wear skin-tone pantyhose? Why not try some of the latest wild colors and patterns that are all the rage? This will pep up your wardrobe without costing a lot of money.

146

If you like to wear ankle highs during the summer, make sure that they really do stay invisible. Wrinkled, skin-colored elasticated bands round your ankles do not look particularly elegant.

Lace is no longer worked on a bobbin nowadays, but made on a loom. Its charm lies in the fact that it leaves what is underneath half seen and half hidden. Good quality lace lingerie is one of the most luxurious types of underwear you could wish for.

147

148

Getting a run in your pantyhose is annoying, but sometimes it happens no matter how careful you are. Always carry a spare pair with you, especially if you are attending an important function.

A bra that is too small will cut into you and cause bulges across your back, ruining your silhouette.

149

White or even very light-colored pantyhose make even the slimmest legs appear fatter than they are. The same applies to light, glossy pantyhose. If the pantyhose is a neutral shade, it will draw less attention to the lower party of your body.

150

151

Small holes which are just starting to run can be treated with (transparent) nail varnish or glue to stop them getting any worse.

152

Opaque pantyhose goes better with flat shoes, whereas the sheer, transparent type should be worn with high heels. If you are buying shoes which you intend to wear with opaque or woolen pantyhose, you need to try the shoes on with this type of pantyhose to avoid ending up with shoes that are too small.

The denier number on the packet indicates the fineness of the yarn. Anything less than 20 denier is very fine and looks very elegant, but is also very fragile.

153

154

Even if you have a small bust which needs no support, you should still wear a stretch top or a bra under clothes that are close-fitting, otherwise your nipples will be too conspicuous.

155

You can extend the life of your stockings and pantyhose by keeping your toenails short and filed smooth. You should also apply cream to your feet to soften any calloused skin which could snag your pantyhose.

When you are putting on your pantyhose, first roll them right down, then carefully draw them over your feet and up to the knee and finally, over your thighs and up to your waist. The material is too delicate to withstand rough treatment.

156

157

Long or jagged fingernails likewise pose a threat to your stockings and pantyhose. You can buy special gloves to wear when taking your pantyhose on and off.

158

If you plan to wear thicker hosiery in winter, then match the color to whatever top you are wearing. For example, a charcoal-gray short-skirted pinstripe suit and red roll neck sweater, calls for red tights and high-legged black boots.

One more tip for prolonging the life of your pantyhose: Avoid shoes that rub because they are too tight or are poorly finished on the inside, as they will inevitably cause snagged threads and lead to runs. Similarly, be careful when zipping up boots.

159

160

Wash fine stockings and pantyhose by hand in lukewarm water using a detergent suitable for delicate fabrics.

161

During the outdoor season, rattan and wicker furniture, as well as other garden furniture, can also pose a danger to fragile stockings and pantyhose. It is almost impossible not to snag them on something and get a run. It is best to avoid wearing your best pantyhose at such an event, or else only go to parties where you'll be standing the whole time.

162

Unless you are wearing trousers, knee-highs look unattractive. No one quite knows why ankle-highs were invented in the first place. They are not even suitable for wearing under trousers since, the moment you sit down, you expose the tops of them along with your bare legs.

163

If you are determined to wash your delicate sheer pantyhose in the washing machine, you must use the program for delicate fabrics and place them in a wash bag. This need be nothing more elaborate than a small retired pillowcase with button fastening.

164

After washing and rinsing, wrap your stockings and your pantyhose in a soft towel and carefully press to remove excess moisture. Then, place them on a fresh, dry towel and leave to dry at room temperature. Never wring, pull, or tug at the material!

165

Hold-ups have a band round the top of each leg which is coated with silicon. It is this silicon layer which holds the stockings in position, but only if it can adhere properly to the skin. In other words, this part of your upper leg must be dry and completely free of grease, so do not use body lotions on this area of your skin.

166

If you have to attend an outdoor meeting in winter, it is better to wear a pantsuit instead of a skirt – with warm woollen stockings underneath. You might just get through the meeting or visit to the construction site without necessarily getting goose pimples.

167

The tumbler is the natural enemy of woolen or wool-mix socks and stockings, and all too often causes shrinkage. Even though it may be more time-consuming, these items should be hung out to dry on the good, old-fashioned washing line.

168

Lingerie made from silk or other delicate materials should always be washed by hand, if at all possible, then rinsed and wrapped in a towel to absorb the worst of the moisture.

169

Before removing any labels sewn into your lingerie because they tickle, scratch, stick up or otherwise irritate, take the trouble to make a note of the washing instructions for each garment. Pin this note up inside your wardrobe or in the vicinity of the washing machine.

170

Wearing pantyhose and trousers at the same time can be an awkward business. Either the trouser leg should be lined on the inside, or the pantyhose should be sheer enough for the trousers to fall smoothly back into position when you get up from a sitting position. Trouser legs which get stuck up around your calves are unattractive and cause embarrassment.

171

You cannot go wrong wearing neutral, unpatterned, skin-toned sheer pantyhose with your business outfits. However, subtle or discreet patterns, which are fairly inconspicuous, are perfectly acceptable. Just avoid any glaringly loud or obtrusive designs.

172

Do not buy any synthetic imitations of woollen pantyhose as these will not keep your legs warm and can cause sweaty feet.

Fishnet stockings and seamed black stockings are not suitable for business wear on account of their questionable erotic overtones. If they happen to become fashionable again and you want to follow the trend, then choose the most expensive and tasteful ones you can afford.

Dark-colored pantyhose with a dark suit? This is carrying sobriety a little too far. Such a combination would be much too gloomy. The only exception to this is wearing black pantyhose with a black outfit to a funeral.

174

175

Do not choose very transparent pantyhose if you are trying to conceal varicose veins. Seek advice as to whether support stockings would be useful in your case. Nowadays, there are many very elegant types on the market, which no longer resemble surgical stockings.

176

Do not store delicate stockings and pantyhose loose in a drawer or cupboard as they are vulnerable to any sharp edges or rough bits of wood. Replace them after use in their original packet or else in a small plastic bag.

Sheer pantyhose, elegant shoes, wintery temperatures – cold feet are a foregone conclusion. Try inserting a wafer thin thermosole inside the shoe.

177

178

Push-up bras are designed with the small to medium-sized bust in mind and may make a naturally bigger bust look too voluptuous.

ACCESSORIES

A few attractive – perhaps even expensive – accessories will provide the finishing touches to a good wardrobe. However, the maxim to remember here is "quality not quantity" and "less is more," otherwise your outfit could easily end up looking too overdone or over-elaborate. Even the smallest accessory is a fashion and style statement in its own right. Never underestimate this effect and choose your "ingredients" with the utmost attention and care.

Accessories are supposed to play a supporting role, not be the main event! They are supposed to go "with" the rest of the outfit. There is no sense in having accessories, for which you first have to purchase an entire outfit and which, after you have worn them, are then likely to disappear to the back of the closet.

179

180

The following rule of thumb applies to accessories: The balance must be right. A heavy tweed suit can stand a sturdy, even largish handbag. A feather-light summer dress, on the other hand, will not look right with anything bulky and is best complemented by a dainty hand-held bag or shoulder bag.

If your fine leather gloves get wet in the rain or snow, never dry them over a direct source of heat (such as a radiator, stove, etc.), but allow them to dry at room temperature. This will help prevent the leather from becoming cracked.

181

182

Rings should not be so tight that they dig into your fingers, making them look fat and sausage-like. Moreover, this could lead to indentations, skin and circulation problems.

A pearl necklace is a classic piece of jewelry which suits all women, goes with every skin tone and flatters any outfit. It does, however, need special care, otherwise it can lose its luster, its legendary mother-of-pearl shimmer. Perfume, hairspray, body lotion, perspiration, makeup and gold or silver chains worn alongside can dull the surface of the pearls, and cause discoloration and scratches.

183

184

Leather wristwatch straps do not last forever, particularly if worn on a daily basis. Get a new strap before the old one begins to look too shabby or breaks.

Shoes with straps tend to create the optical effect of making the legs look shorter. Choose a style that has the strap as low down the foot as possible, in other words, across the instep rather than the ankle. Any straps should also be narrow with quite an inconspicuous buckle fastening.

185

186

Long, dangling earrings help to slim down a roundish face. Any ear jewelry that is designed in the shape of balls or circles should be avoided at all costs.

187

Eyeglasses should also be regarded as an accessory that adds to the overall look. Choose a pair of frames which suit the shape of your face: Square-shaped frames suit round faces, large, wide frames look good on longish faces, square-shaped faces look best with round styles and oval faces can wear just about any style.

It is not only the style of the handbag, but also its size that you must take into consideration. Tiny little bags look just as silly on tall women as suitcase-sized ones on petite women.

188

189

If costume jewelry causes your skin to break out in an itchy rash, you are probably allergic to the nickel content. Consult your doctor. If this diagnosis is confirmed, you should only ever wear the real article, or else ensure that your costume jewelry is nickel-free and hypoallergenic.

However hard it may be, allow your favorite shoes at least one day's rest after each wearing so that the leather gets a chance to dry out and recover.

190

Sweaters are not just for pulling on, they can also serve as accessories. Throw a fine sweater made of pure new wool or cashmere round your shoulders, or tie it round your waist or hips.

191

192

Shoes which have a dark toecap, like Chanel's famous two-tone shoes, make a long foot seem shorter and daintier.

193

Accessories made of synthetic material are not necessarily easier to care for. Be it a fun plastic ring or your precious Swatch, the materials can be susceptible to scratches. Skin creams and cleansing lotions can also make them look dull.

194

Be careful when buying shoes: If you are unsure whether the heel is too high for you, then it probably is too high. However, anyone who is used to wearing shoes with heels, and has no problem walking in them, will very quickly get used to wearing shoes with really high heels.

195

A pair of pearl ear studs looks sophisticated, but out of place with a sporty look, such as a sweater and jeans.

Instead of knotting a silk scarf round your neck, you can hold it in place using a proper scarf ring, easily available in any accessories boutique. You will find it keeps even very voluminous scarves neater and under control.

197 196

Be wary of gold, white, metallic-colored, or leopard skin-type shoes. They are almost impossible to integrate into any stylish outfit. You may find these styles making an appearance as a passing fashion trend, but they will almost certainly be unwearable the following season.

Many women rely on an appointments diary in calendar form or a page-a-day diary. If you would feel completely lost without your "second memory," at least treat yourself to a good one. Cheap plastic diaries advertising the name of the company which gave them away as a free gift are pretty tasteless.

198

199

If you become the victim of a burglary or a fire, you may find that your jewelry is insufficiently covered by your current household contents insurance. Heirlooms, in particular, may be worth a great deal to you, but the sums paid out in compensation could be relatively insignificant. Make inquiries with your insurance company. It may be wise to take out an additional policy.

You can store your fur coat with a furrier during the summer season. He will also ensure that it is brought out and prepared in good time, ready for you to wear as soon as winter sets in again.

200

201

If you bring your new conquest home with you, do not immediately throw off your shoes and change into your slippers. Unless, of course, a cucumber face mask is more what you have in mind.

Do not try to compete with your daughter. Rucksacks are a prerogative of youth and look too contrived with an outfit worn by a more mature woman. Conversely, daughters should not try and compete with their mothers. The elegant Hermès purse belonging to mom may well look very sophisticated, but it does not go very well with jeans and sneakers.

202

203

If you must have one of the popular designer bags, then buy an original Vuitton, or Gucci or Prada or whatever you have set your heart on, but leave the cheap imitations offered by market traders well alone. Imitations are embarrassing and will ruin your image – and more people than you think can spot this sort of trash a mile off.

Have your pearl necklace checked over once a year. It is better to have it rethreaded than to wait until it weakens and breaks, possibly losing a few pearls in the process.

204

Take a pair of your own socks with you when trying on shoes. You can then be sure that your feet do not come into contact with shoes that other people have tried on before you. Do not try on shoes in your bare feet – not just for reasons of hygiene, but also because you will not get an accurate idea of the fit or shape of the shoe in question.

205

206

The rule about not wearing genuine jewelry at the same time as costume jewelry has long since been superseded. It is now acceptable to wear any combination you feel like. The main thing is that the pieces go well together in terms of style.

207

Have you been searching for a specific color of scarf to go with one particular coat, suit, or pullover? Or were the scarves you saw too expensive? Visit a good fabric store and explore the range of soft, colored materials available. You will need at least one square yard of material, more if you want a particularly large scarf. Once you get home, you can neaten up the edges or ask your dressmaker to do this for you.

208

Send your jewelry regularly to the jeweler's. He will expertly remove any dirt which may have accumulated in the tiniest cracks and crevices as a result of perspiration, skin cream, dust etc., polish away any scratches and try to remove discoloration and repair any damage. Rest assured that your precious pieces will shine and sparkle like new.

209

Just for a change, fold your silk scarf into a band and wear it as a belt or sash. When buying a scarf, ask for a leaflet illustrating the different ways of wearing it. Entire books are now available devoted to this subject.

210

Buy yourself a good umbrella. Cheap ones, which turn you into a walking advertisement, are not compatible with good style. A classic, handmade, good quality umbrella will give you years of pleasure and be a worthwhile investment – provided, of course, you do not forget it somewhere.

211

Match your metal belt buckle to any gold or silver elements in the rest of the accessories you may be wearing. Gold with gold, silver with silver. This will look really stylish.

You have inherited some accessories, but do not like wearing them? Maybe the mink stole, string of pearls, or wristwatch do not really suit your style? Do not be in too much of a hurry. Perhaps it is too soon after the bereavement for you to regard the items as your own. On no account should you throw or give them away. The embroidered bag may well skip a generation and become your daughter's, niece's, or granddaughter's most precious possession.

212

An expensive fountain pen or an exclusive writing set are wonderful accessories which ought to be used, even if they might easily get lost or stolen. To give maximum pleasure, writing equipment should be kept in constant use, otherwise pens will dry up and no longer write fluently.

213

214

If worn for too long, ear clips can begin to pinch painfully. Try to stick to the type of clips that have little silicon pads on the inside. If you are really fond of ear jewelry, you should think seriously about having your ears pierced. This will save you the inconvenience of uncomfortable clips.

If you feel constricted by classic-style belts, why not try a chain belt. Many belts of this kind are easily adjustable to the correct length. If worn loosely around the hips, it will bring a swing to your step, without it being too tight or restrictive.

215

216

Knee-length boots are chic and give an impression of long, slim legs – but only if the boots are a close fit and do not gape away from the leg, otherwise the effect will be the opposite.

217

Just because your whole outfit is black, this does not automatically mean that you have to wear black shoes and carry a black handbag. Why not experiment a little with different-colored accessories. A combination of black and dark blue can also look very sophisticated.

218

Wristwatches, too, should be purchased with a view to your overall proportions. Very small ones look particularly good on petite women. They would be lost, however, on a large woman. A big watch on a thin wrist looks as if you have borrowed it from your "big sister."

Store your jewelry in a padded jewelry box containing as many compartments as possible. This will help prevent it becoming scratched or damaged in any way.

219

220

Brand name jewelry from a particular jewelry firm, such as Cartier, has a higher resale value than other no-name products, should you ever have to or want to part with it. Whatever happens, retain your certificate of sale in a safe place. Jewelry should never be seen as an investment, however, as experience shows that the price you can expect for secondhand pieces is very low.

Special padded insoles will give your feet support, even in high-heeled shoes, and will help keep your toes from pressing too far forward and eventually causing pain and discomfort.

221

222

Where to wear your belt? Waist belts can be shorter than hip belts, which need to be a few holes longer. It is a good idea to try belts on before you buy.

223

You have treated yourself to an elegant cashmere scarf. That's great, so make sure you wear it, preferably every day! Do not try to save your best accessories for the proverbial "special occasion." They are there to give you pleasure, not to be left languishing in a cardboard box.

224

If you want to make the most of a particularly striking accessory, such as an unusual ring, an exclusive necklace, or an over-the-top but pretty brooch, then wear your eye-catching piece on its own, without any other ornamentation, to complement a neutral self-colored outfit.

225

Sometimes you have a favorite pair of shoes that you would like to go on wearing year after year. Eventually, however, the shape of the heel is going to go out of fashion. What do you do with them? Throw them away? Store your beloved shoes up in the attic? Send them for recycling? Certainly not! Talk to your local shoe-repairer. It is quite possible that he will be able to replace the heels with new, more up-to-date ones.

SMALL BUDGET –
BIG IMPACT

Good taste does not have to cost a great deal – and, conversely, a large amount of money will not automatically secure you an exquisite wardrobe. A few little tricks can considerably reduce the cost of an outfit without having to compromise on style. You have to be able to make the distinction, however, between the areas of your wardrobe where you can indeed make a few savings and others where only top quality will do.

226

No one needs a massive wardrobe full of expensive clothes. Fill it instead with timeless basics which you can pep up with fashionable accessories. In this way, you can keep up easily with any fashion trends that appeal to you without having to re-stock your entire wardrobe every season.

Before setting off on your shopping trip, you should give careful thought to how much money you have available to spend. Then, with that in mind, look specifically for items that are within your means. Be firm about avoiding expensive goods.

227

228

Blouses, jackets and coats often have a little bag attached containing spare buttons. Do not throw this away, but keep them all together in a special button box. You are bound to need one or two of them some day.

To get the maximum effect from a minimal budget, make black the basic color of your whole wardrobe. It always looks sophisticated. Black clothes usually look expensive even if they were not. Black also has a slimming effect. There are no color-coordinating problems, as you can team anything with anything. You only need to buy your accessories once (shoes, scarf, gloves etc.). Black clothes do not have to keep being cleaned all the time.

229

230

Moths feed on material, and can make quite a hole in your clothes budget! Take the precaution of lining your closets with moth-repellent paper (checking the sell-by date regularly) and/or cedarwood blocks.

Everyone makes a bad buy sometimes. Do not waste time getting upset about it, but try to work out what it is that you dislike about the new garment, what made you buy it in the first place, and how you could shop more effectively in future.

231

232

A good dressmaker who can do alterations can be very useful in getting your clothes to fit perfectly. But how do you know if the little workshop round the corner is any good? If you have not been there before, test it first with a garment that you are not so attached to. Whatever you do, do not experiment with your favorite outfit or an expensive new acquisition.

If you have a small budget, the main thing is to shop only for what you need. Ten bargain buys, which do not even go together and which you will soon tire of anyway, simply means wasted money.

233

No matter how temptingly low the price is, try on each item before buying it. Do not spend money on items reduced by 50 percent if you are not 100 percent sure that they fit you.

234

235

Think carefully before trying to deal with a serious stain yourself. If your efforts do not work, most dry cleaners will be reluctant or even refuse to accept an article of clothing with a mark that has been inexpertly tampered with.

You would dearly love the status of owning an accessory by Vuitton, Hermes, Gucci, or one of the other famous labels, even though such a thing is really beyond your means. Okay, but do not be tempted to go for the cheapest item of the whole range, which proclaims to everyone that "this is the best I could afford." Save up for an extra month and buy yourself a senior and more mid-range model. After all, you'll be wearing it for a good few years to come.

If your preference is for shirt-style blouses with turned-back cuffs, you can buy little braided silk knots in every conceivable color as a cheap, but very pretty, alternative to expensive gold or silver cuff links.

238 237

Take any quartz watches which have stopped working straight to a watch repairer. If you do not replace the battery quickly, it may begin to leak and ruin the watch.

239

Even the most expensive outfit in the world will not create a stunning image if the wearer has neglected to take care of herself. A hairstyle that is in need of a fresh cut, or possibly no hairstyle at all, bad skin, dirty fingernails, yellow teeth, body odors would all ruin the effect of the outfit. Conversely, an immaculately groomed woman will look sophisticated and attractive even in inexpensive clothes. So, get yourself up to scratch first, before turning your attention to your wardrobe.

240

Some boutiques really do treat customers with condescension, as if they are doubtful as to whether "she can actually afford that." However much you may wish to prove that you do have the necessary purchasing power, never let yourself be goaded into a spontaneous purchase. Unfortunately, it is your money that would be wasted, not that of the salesclerk.

241

Do not spend money on a fashion trend that has nearly had its day. If you want to buy something really up-to-the-minute, watch out for new fashions that you are likely to be able to wear for longer than just one season.

Even if those pale blue slippers embossed with pink diamanté are the latest word in fashion, take heed: If your wardrobe consists predominantly of natural colors, leave well alone!

242

243

Choose a headband or hair band to match the color of the rest of your outfit, thus avoiding any clash of colors and producing a general effect that is perfectly coordinated. Such attention to detail creates a sophisticated and elegant impression – and costs little enough to achieve.

Light-colored leather gloves become soiled and grubby-looking very quickly, but this is no reason to discard them. Special shampoo for leather gloves is available from specialist stores. Your good gloves will not necessarily seem like new, but will definitely look considerably smarter. Besides, leather benefits from looking a little worn.

244

245

Wristwatches in trendy colors may be very chic, but do tend to restrict what you wear. Unless you can run to dozens of different watches, you would be well advised to stick to one with a brown or black strap. A two-tone stainless steel watch bracelet that will go with both gold and silver jewellery is also a very wise choice.

246

The straps on shoulder bags should
be the correct length for your height,
or should be adjustable so that they
do not hang down around your calves
or up under your armpit (unless of
course that is what you want).

247

In order to keep the inside of your wardrobe fresh-smelling and ensure that your clothes always smell pleasant when you come to wear them, you should, if at all possible, always keep worn clothes separate from unworn ones. Only keep clean and washed clothes in the wardrobe. This will also help keep moths at bay.

It is difficult to throw things away, particularly if you have a tight budget. But no matter how expensive that blazer was, or how exclusive the shop where you purchased those shoes, anything you no longer need or like should be discarded.

248

249

Care for your leather hand-bag as carefully as you do your shoes. This keeps the leather looking its best for as long as possible. Use a shoe-cleaning product sold by a specialist shop or a good quality shoe cream. Test the product on an inconspicuous part of the bag.

250

If you have a cigarette burn, moth holes, or a small tear in the fabric where you snagged it somewhere, take the damaged outfit to a professional who specializes in invisible mending. Such things can often be repaired.

251

Are you looking for something to team with a particular item of clothing? It is a good idea to wear the garment when trying on potential buys, or at least take it with you, when you go on your shopping trip.

252

A stubborn stain, which is still clearly visible even after several washes, can sometimes be concealed by a bit of embroidery or an appliquéd motif. A brooch, or pinned-on flower can also be useful camouflage.

You do not need to spend a fortune on accessories. A charming evening bag from the flea market, a pretty necklace of paste stones, a classic Swatch will serve the same purpose. The important thing is that it should be exactly right for you, your style, and the outfit you are wearing.

253

254

Does the color of this blouse go with these trousers? Ask a sales assistant to let you see the item in daylight. Colors that harmonize in the artificial light of the boutique may well clash horribly in natural sunlight.

255

Do not let yourself be seduced by a low price in the end-of-season sales. Ask yourself whether the item would have tempted you if it had been twice the price. If the answer is no, then leave it, regardless of how cheap it is.

Carry out a regular inspection of your wardrobe, casting a critical eye over its contents. Any clothes that you no longer wear, or perhaps have never worn, are good candidates for the secondhand store. The money you get for them there can be used to buy a classic garment that you really like.

256

257

Many clothes remain unworn because the hem is hanging down, a seam has come adrift, or the zipper has become stuck. Either get down to some mending yourself or have them repaired.

258

If you want to prolong the life of your shoes, treat yourself to a shoe tree. Any creases in the leather resulting from the natural flexing of your feet can be smoothed out in this way and the shoes will retain their overall shape.

259

Know exactly what you are looking for when you go bargain-hunting in the sales. You can often buy top-of-the-range clothes at bargain prices. Sales usually begin well before the official start time, however, so make an early start to ensure you get the maximum choice.

260

Take care if you are shopping abroad. In some countries, value-added tax is not included in the price. It is not necessarily shown on the price tag and the first you know of it is when you get to the checkout.

You have decided to turn a long skirt into a trendy miniskirt. Ask your dressmaker to allow for a generous hem just in case you ever want to lengthen it again, if you get fed up with the short look.

261

262

Do not cut corners when it comes to having expensive silk scarves dry-cleaned. If necessary, ask a good store or dressmaker to recommend a dry-cleaner. If you wash them at home by hand, the colors may run.

263

If you want to negotiate a price in a store, then do so in a friendly and polite manner. Any unrealistic demands are likely to fall on deaf ears. Never ask for ridiculously large discounts.

264

Never accept soiled goods, even if the salesgirl swears on her grandmother's life that the little mark is merely dust and is sure to come out. If the mark doesn't come out, you will have great difficulty exchanging the item once it has been washed or cleaned in vain.

Some woolens are prone to pilling, especially where the surfaces rub together. The little bits of wool can be shaved off with a special wool razor, but an ordinary razor can do the job just as well.

265

266

Sometimes it is only when you get home that you can tell whether your new clothes go with the clothes already in your wardrobe. Exchange anything you are not happy with at the earliest opportunity or take advantage of the money-back guarantee, if there is one. Always keep your receipts.

You do not own any expensive jewelry. Never mind! Necks and wrists weighted down with too much jewelry are definitely "out" anyway. One single piece, such as a chain, wristwatch or a ring, is more than enough.

267

Twinsets are available in all sorts of different shapes and materials – and you get three outfits in one: a pullover, a jacket and a combination of the two. Go and get yourself one!

268

269

Think long and hard before deciding to have a tattoo, not just because of the financial outlay. Even with the advent of laser technology, it is not all that easy to remove a tattoo, if one day you decide you do not like it anymore. One alternative is to get a temporary or self-adhesive tattoo, although these can sometimes cause an allergic reaction.

It is not only clothes that appreciate a little tender loving care. Your wardrobe will also enjoy a good clean occasionally. This helps to keep the contents fresh for longer.

270

271

Secondhand stores are the perfect destination for a shopping trip on a small budget. Nowadays there are also stores that sell secondhand designer clothes, some of which have only been worn once. If you do not like the idea of wearing other people's clothes, look for secondhand accessories such as expensive handbags or fashion jewelry.

HANDY HINTS FOR PACKING AND TRAVELING

Travel has nowadays become an integral part of our lives. In addition to vacations, many women now travel and fly regularly as part of their working calendar. This repeatedly raises the question of what to pack and how to travel as lightly as possible. It goes without saying that we want to look good while we are away, without having to carry a lot of unnecessary baggage around with us.

On long flights, it helps to have a comfort pack with you containing thick, warm socks, so that you can take your tight shoes off without getting cold feet, a warm cardigan or large wrap to protect against the cold air-conditioning, and a moisturizing cream to combat the effects of dry air.

272

273

When traveling, take a minimum amount of jewelry with you. Check before you leave which pieces go with which outfit and leave the rest at home.

274

A reversible belt, brown on one side, black on the other, is an ideal travel accessory. The black side will go with your black business shoes, while the brown side will perfectly complement your leisure wear.

275

Many cosmetics are now available in handy travel packs. This saves on space and weight. If you are staying away for any length of time, it may be better to buy yourself a simple shampoo or sunblock once you reach your destination, instead of buying these items at home and dragging them along.

If you are taking a beach holiday and staying in a middle-class hotel, you can wear what you like. But, please, do not turn up in the restaurant half-naked: Slip a lightweight dress, or trousers and T-shirt, over your swimsuit or bikini.

276

277

A holiday in a four-star or luxury hotel calls for a bit of care with regard to choosing which clothes to take – not to mention a large suitcase. Beach wear really should be restricted to the beach or pool area. You will need presentable dresses or suits to wear for lunch and more elegant outfits for dinner. Do not forget to take a cocktail dress or evening dress for gala occasions.

If you are on your way to an important business meeting or private function, try to pack your "official" wardrobe in your hand luggage, if possible. Suitcases always seem to go missing or arrive late for the very occasions when you need them most.

278

In some countries, it is customary for a visitor to remove his shoes on entering somebody's home. Make sure that your socks or pantyhose are clean and presentable.

279

280

Before you travel, check that your outfits are in good condition. It is better to use the right thread before you leave home, rather than end up having to do an emergency repair with thread of dubious quality from the hotel's sewing kit.

281

You prefer not to take additional free-time clothes with you on your business trip, but would still like to wear something a little more informal once your meetings are over. Substitute your elegant blouse for a sporty shirt and replace your suit jacket with a pullover or cardigan.

If you have a long journey ahead of you, wait until the very last minute, if you can, before wearing your business outfit. In summer, especially, it is pleasant not to arrive in sweaty, crumpled clothes. If you are staying overnight, you may be able to get changed in your hotel room prior to your meeting. If you have no opportunity whatsoever to change your outfit, then at least hang up your jacket on a hanger in the back of the car.

282

283

Have you been invited for a weekend visit and do not know what sort of clothes to take with you? Ask your hosts quite openly what activities they have planned (horse-riding, hiking, rough and tumble with the kids, dinner at home or out in a restaurant, an evening at the opera?) and find out what kind of dress code is required. This does not indicate a lack of confidence or imagination on your part, but merely underlines your desire to dress appropriately out of respect for your hosts.

"Will you tidy up that closet!" Does this injunction bring back memories of childhood? Even if you still feel that tidying up is a nuisance, you must grit your teeth and find some time for this chore occasionally. A tidy closet, with everything in its place, will save you a lot of time when you are packing.

284

285

Hand luggage is very useful and you should make full use of it. Any valuables and important documents should be kept with you when traveling and not be entrusted to a suitcase. Any personal travel or I.D. documents, cash, checks, credit cards, as well as any medication that you take regularly should be carried in your hand luggage, as well as any valuable or treasured jewelry.

286

If you are going on a traditional type of cruise or traveling by ship, you will require an extensive wardrobe, which includes evening clothes, as well as whatever outfits might be needed to suit the different climates of the places you are visiting ashore. Find out beforehand what is the usual dress code on board your ship.

The shoulder of a jacket is usually the most vulnerable part of it. To avoid it looking crumpled when you get it out of the suitcase, you can pad it out with socks, underwear, or rolled-up T-shirts.

287

288

Suitcases with a dividing panel and elastic straps will at least hold the contents in place to some extent. Before investing in a new suitcase, check out the interior carefully.

289

When packing a travel bag, place
heavy items, such as shoes, jeans and
thick sweaters, at the bottom and
delicate items like blouses on top.

Linen is well known for being extremely prone to creasing. It is only at its best when it is hanging freshly ironed in your wardrobe. Nothing could be worse for linen than being squashed in a bulging suitcase or a narrow airplane seat. If you are determined to take linen garments with you, you should think about investing in a small travel iron.

290

291

A pair of old gloves kept in the car – or, if you prefer, a pair of special driving gloves – can prove invaluable in protecting your freshly manicured hands from getting splashed with gasoline, or covered with the smell of fuel oil and windshield dirt, when you stop at the service station on your way to work or setting off on a business trip.

Some hotels offer rooms with an iron, or else keep such items available for guests to borrow. Inquire about this when making your reservations. It may be possible to have items ironed by the hotel's own laundry service.

292

Suits made from high-quality material are ideal for journeys and holidays. Wool, cashmere, mohair, or mixtures of any of these, can be packed in a suitcase with little ill effect. A small amount of additional synthetic material makes them even more crease-resistant.

293

294

Be wary of the shoe-cleaning machines you find in nearly every hotel, especially if you are wearing light-colored shoes. These machines are mainly used by men in brown brogues or stout black shoes. You can never be sure, therefore, when you get your squirt of neutral polish on the polishing brush, that your light shoes will not end up covered in dark blotches.

295

Every inch of space counts. Fill the cavities of shoes with socks, pantyhose, woolen gloves, or other soft accessories. This also has the added advantage of helping your shoes keep their shape.

296

If one of your favorite holiday activities is shopping, it might be a good idea to pack a spare bag, which folds flat, so that your suitcase is not filled to bursting with new items on your return trip.

297

Hang any items which crease easily on hangers next to your suitcase, ready to be packed at the very last minute. When you reach your destination, unpack them as soon as possible, and leave anything else that will not come to any harm in your suitcase, until you have recovered somewhat from the exertions of the journey.

298

Steam is useful for getting rid of creases. Take a hot shower, or fill a bathtub with hot water until the windows, mirror, and tiles are completely steamed up. Then hang up your clothes in this tropical climate. Next morning, your clothes will be fresh, neat, and uncreased.

The perfect suitcase has yet to be invented. Every model has its own particular advantages and disadvantages. Rigid suitcases are good for plane journeys as they can withstand pretty rough treatment. Unfortunately, they are also heavy and not particularly attractive. Leather cases are elegant but vulnerable and require a great deal of maintenance. Nylon suitcases are extremely light and can stretch a little to accommodate a last minute item. On the negative side, however, they do not offer much protection against knocks or heavy rain.

300

Perhaps you are traveling in your own car and have all kinds of room in the trunk. That's great! You can take whatever you want. It is fun to have a choice of clothes available when you get to your destination. And who knows, the sun may well be shining in one city, while another disappears under a blanket of snow.

301

Before embarking on your trip abroad, make inquiries about any traditions and customs in the country you are about to visit. This includes any special rules about clothes. Read a good travel guide or, if the region is not on the usual tourist track, ask the consulate for information.

302

Dark blue, black or charcoal-gray basics are ideal clothes for traveling in, as they do not need to be constantly washed or dry-cleaned. Even the worst horrors, such as red wine or soya sauce stains, can go virtually unnoticed on these colors.

Regardless of which country you are visiting, if you are planning to visit a holy shrine, never ever do so in beach clothes or swimwear.

303

304

Brightly colored plastic money belts, which keep your money and valuables safe from thieves while you are on holiday, may well be practical, but are unattractive and unflattering. One alternative is to have a small purse for essentials, which will tuck into your pocket, and to leave the rest of your valuables in the hotel safe. This is an equally effective method of theft prevention.

Beauty tips

Being well-dressed is just one side of the fashion coin, the other side is looking after your skin and hair. Equal attention must be devoted to both these aspects in order to achieve an elegant appearance. Good personal hygiene and the use of cosmetics should be second nature to every woman. What is important in this respect is not so much the perennial fight against lines and wrinkles but simply to look one's best and feel fresh and attractive.

The shade of makeup you use must be exactly right for your complexion. Testing a little bit on the back of your hand under the artificial light of the department store is no good whatsoever. Visit a beautician and test different shades on your face and look at them in both artificial light and daylight. It will be worth the extra expense.

305

306

Body odor is very embarrassing as well as bad for the environment. Always use an effective deodorant.

The color of people's teeth varies from one individual to another. Blue-toned lipsticks, such as violet or pink, are only suitable for those with very white teeth. If your teeth tend to be yellowish (as the majority of teeth are), you should stick to lipsticks in shades of red or brown.

307

308

Nail polish will last longer if the nails are dry (so do not apply it right after a shower) and free of grease (do not use any moisturizing creams beforehand). A layer of special "undercoat" will also help to keep the nail color intact for longer.

309

Reduce the amount of jewelry you wear. Wearing heavyweight gold chains will age you ten years.

310

If your hair is quick to go greasy at the roots, while the ends tend to be on the dry side, you should apply hair-enriching products or conditioners in such a way that they target the areas that need them most, leaving the roots and scalp untouched.

Do you suffer from dry, tight skin after a long shower? Apply a moisturizing cream to your face beforehand.

311

312

Black makes you look slimmer, but not necessarily beautiful. Anything dark, particularly near your face, absorbs the light and can make you appear pale.

Makeup can only be applied evenly over smooth, immaculate skin. Treat your face to regular cleansing by a professional.

313

314

Sprouting underarm hair is not only unattractive, but also encourages body odor. A razor and a good depilatory cream will take care of this problem.

315

One perfume a day is sufficient, so stick to it and do not spray on another one later (unless you have had a shower and are changing clothes) as this will create a indefinable muddle of fragrances. Take care that your deodorant is gentle, neutral and, if possible, fragrance-free, so that it does not clash with your favorite perfume.

Cosmetics do not keep forever and old makeup can cause skin irritation. Sift through your cosmetic drawer at regular intervals and discard any old tubes and pots. Creams with a high water content will keep for three months, whereas normal creams last six months. Lipsticks stay fresh for about a year.

316

317

Hairy legs on women are not everyone's cup of tea, either bare or in pantyhose. Keep your skin smooth by means of regular shaving, depilatory creams, or wax and other similar treatments.

If you are prone to allergic reactions and skin irritations, make sure you test any cosmetics you are using for the first time on a small patch of skin on the inside of your wrist, on your neck, or any other sensitive area. If there is no adverse reaction within 24 hours, you can risk using the product.

318

319

Too much mascara makes your eyelashes stick together unattractively or coagulates into unsightly blobs. Separate the individual lashes using an eyelash brush or comb.

Untended hands and peeling nail polish make a very poor impression. For a mini-manicure, clean under the edge of your nails, cut them all to the same length (even if this means relatively short) and always use hand cream to keep your hands soft.

320

321

A cloud of perfume that you can smell a mile away is too pervasive. Be economical in your use of it and only use Eau de Toilette or Eau de Cologne in the daytime. Save your highly concentrated Eau de Parfum for the evening.

Eyeliner is now in fashion again, but it is difficult for an unpracticed hand to apply it successfully. For best results, rest both elbows on a solid surface when applying eyeliner. This will reduce the wobble factor. Starting in the inner corner of the eye and moving outwards, apply it in one smooth motion along the edge of your lid just above the eyelashes.

Investing in a discreet permanent makeup treatment can sometimes be a good thing – but only if it is done perfectly. Make inquiries about the institute in question before you commit yourself and ask your skin specialist or beautician. Bear in mind, too, that unforeseen skin reactions may occur. To be absolutely safe, it is better to avoid such measures altogether.

323

324

Plucking your eyebrows opens up the area around your eyes and draws attention to them, as well as presenting a more well-groomed appearance than untamed bushy hair growth. Follow the natural line of your eyebrows and only pluck the lower edge of the brow so that the result is not too dramatic.

325

Make sure you have the right tools for your day-to-day hair care. Cheap plastic combs or brushes often have sharp edges which can cause damage to your hair. Handmade horn combs and brushes with natural bristles cannot be too highly recommended. They may be more expensive, but will last forever. And your hair will thank you.

Does your hair always seem tired and limp? Do you get one "bad hair day" after another? It is possible that you have used too many products on your hair. Avoid using hair treatments, hair rinses, or styling products too often as these can cause your hair to lose its vitality. Special cleansing shampoos are available, which can eliminate the effects of too many hair-care products.

326

327

If you suffer from serious skin problems, such as acne, skin infections, allergies, or very dry, itchy skin, do not spend months working your way through all the cosmetics on the shelves of the drugstore, but make an appointment at the earliest opportunity with a dermatologist. He will give you the medication you need and your skin will soon be restored to perfect health again.

328

Finding the right colors to suit your face is one thing, but applying them correctly is another. If you are not happy with your makeup skills or want to learn how to make more of yourself, consult a makeup specialist and ask her to show you a few makeup tricks.

329

Long hair is great for turning heads, but it can sometimes be a real nuisance. Ask your hairdresser to show you how to pin it up in an upswept hairstyle. The main thing is to learn exactly how it is done so that you can copy the look yourself at home.

330

If you have a lot of unwanted hair on your upper lip, cheeks, or chin, it may be worth having this unwanted growth removed permanently by someone professionally trained in this field. The procedure may be rather expensive, but you will be free of the problem once and for all and will no longer have to suffer all that painful plucking.

331

You arrive home after a long, exciting evening and all you want to do is fall into bed and sleep. Before you can do so, however, you must remove all traces of your makeup and apply your usual skin-care cream, even if this takes your last ounce of strength. Your skin will be able to breathe and the woman you will come face to face with in the bathroom mirror in a few hours' time will not look half so bad.

Your nails simply refuse to grow into long, slim claws. So what? Most elegant women wear their fingernails short. The natural look is best for well-manicured nails.

332

333

Your morning beauty routine can become quite boring after a while, and special treatments like manicures, polishing fingernails, having a pedicure, applying a face mask, and undergoing hair treatments take time. Keep yourself entertained by listening to music or watching TV, or bury yourself in a good book. Change the product you use from time to time. Looking after yourself should be fun.

334

Perfume and sunshine are not compatible. You run the risk of developing spots, rashes, and unfortunate skin discoloration. It is advisable to leave the perfume until after the sun has set. Alternatively, you can resort to special products that tolerate sun.

335

If you swim in the open sea or in the swimming pool, give your hair a thorough rinse afterwards in clean water to remove all traces of salt or chlorine which can be damaging.

Suntan lotion and any other UV protection products that you have brought back from holiday can be used up as body lotion. They will not keep until next year anyway.

336

337

A bath can be very relaxing and beneficial. But the water temperature should not be more than 100 °F (38 °C) and you should not remain in the bath for longer than 15–20 minutes as this could put too much strain on your circulation and dehydrate the skin.

Bronzing face powder is an alternative to foundation cream and helps give your complexion a fresh, sun-tanned look. Brush it lightly over your face and neck with a soft, thick brush, but be careful not to apply too much of it.

338

339

If you have sensitive eyes, which easily become bloodshot and are prone to infection, or if you wear contact lenses, you should use special eye makeup products that are hypoallergenic and have been clinically tested and declared safe.

340

Rough elbows can be softened by rubbing the hard skin with two halves of a freshly cut lemon after showering. The only way to keep this area of your skin permanently soft and smooth is to moisturize regularly with skin cream.

341

Delicate, light colors for lipstick, eye shadow and rouge will produce a natural look and are ideal for daytime makeup. Pastel pink will make tired eyes look brighter in the morning.

342

Great care must also be taken of the area around your neckline, as the skin here is particularly delicate and quick to show wrinkles and lines. This delicate area needs pampering with the same products you use on your face.

343

Fresh breath is vital. Clean your teeth at least twice a day, use a mouthwash and/or dental floss. Suck peppermints to freshen your breath if you are on the go for any length of time and, of course, have regular checkups with your dentist.

A wan, pallid complexion is often a sign of poor circulation. Use a peel-off face pack to suit your skin type and rub your face afterwards with a large ice cube to encourage circulation. Try to take more exercise in the fresh air as this will also put the rose back in your cheeks.

344

345

A combination skin is not always easy to deal with, but special dual-action products are available, which are designed to cope with the oily skin around the forehead, nose and chin (T-zone) and dry skin on the cheeks. Bear in mind the different needs of each area: An intensive facial mask treatment should only be carried out on the T-zone, while the cheeks would benefit more from an enriching mask.

346

Brush your teeth once a week with ordinary household salt. This will help prevent discoloration and staining.

347

Remove makeup gently. Too much rubbing or rough handling can cause fine lines to appear in the thin, delicate skin around the eyes.

348

Lipstick looks best on smooth lips. Remove any traces of loose skin regularly by gentle brushing with a toothbrush. Apply a lip balm afterwards.

The sort of narrow shoes currently in fashion increase the risk of developing painful ingrowing toenails. Trim your nails regularly and walk around the house in bare or stocking feet.

349

350

The best way to cleanse delicate skin is by using special pH neutral products and cleansing lotions. You may wish to consult a dermatologist to ascertain exactly which is the right product for your particular skin type.

351

Drinking plenty of fluids not only benefits the kidneys, but also keeps your skin firm and vital. Try to drink at least four, if not six, pints of mineral water, fruit juice or unsweetened fruit or herbal tea a day. This takes a good deal of discipline at first, but is basically just a question of habit.

352

Are you trying to cultivate beautiful long fingernails? Apply a tough clear nail polish to the top and underneath of your nails to make them stronger.

353

If you are planning to wage war against cellulite, what you need above anything else is perseverance and determination. There are no miracle cures, but a combination of healthy eating, exercise, such as cycling or walking, regular massages, firming beauty products, and specially targeted gymnastic exercises will contribute to a marked improvement.

354

During the cold winter months, you may find that your hair is often affected by static electricity, making it stick out in all directions. Dry winter air, too much central heating, and thick clothing are all contributing factors to this phenomenon. Dampen your comb or brush with water before styling your hair or rub a little hair cream into your hair with the palm of your hand.

Before deciding on a drastic change of hair color, bear in mind that the roots will need to be redyed every four to six weeks. Roots that are in need of redoing look just as unattractive as a perm that is growing out.

355

356

Varicose veins are not just an unsightly cosmetic problem, but can be a medical one, too. Consult a specialist about the possibility of having them removed.

357

Once you reach a certain age, a mane of raven black hair looks rather unnatural. Either let your gray streaks show or change to a softer, more natural shade of hair color.

358

Hair covered with dandruff creates a very poor impression. If you cannot get rid of the dandruff with the special brands of shampoo, consult a pharmacist, or visit a dermatologist.

359

Braids are not a suitable hairstyle for a mature woman who wants to be taken seriously, and are best left to young girls who look cute and appealing with this type of hairstyle.

Give your fingernails a little rest from nail polish now and again. Instead, polish them to a shine with a special nail buffer.

360

361

Shiny, oily areas of skin on your face can be treated with special tissues, with which you can dab the skin during the day to stop it looking shiny. Using makeup specially designed for oily skin will also help.

362

Intensive exercise and dieting might make your legs slimmer, but not longer. The best way to get around this is to wear high-heeled shoes.

363

You want a shade of lipstick that is right for all situations and goes with every outfit? Choose one of the rosewood shades.

Rings under your eyes should be covered at all costs using an appropriate camouflage stick. Otherwise, those dark shadows will mar the entire effect of your makeup, and make you look tired and washed-out.

364

365

No matter how much importance is attached nowadays to beauty and to clothes, never lose sight of the fact that these are, after all, merely superficial attributes and there really are far more important things in life.

Illustrations:

Amadeus Fashion, Austria (173), Belvest S.p.A., Italy (3, 11), Betty Barcley, Germany (38, 61), Cartier, France (113, 198, 236, 315), Etienne Aigner AG, Germany (48, 148, 159, 211), Fratelli Rossetti, Italy (96, 179, 359), Hilton Vestimenta, Italy (130, 225, 289, 304, 322), JOOP! GmbH, Germany (36, 77, 102, 104, 135, 137, 267), Laura Camino, Spain (endpapers, 110, 246), Les Copains, Italy (60, 68, 83, 166, 187, 325, 341, 349), Loro Piana, Italy (23, 58, 89, 223, 229, 256), Louis Vuitton, France (203, 278), Officine Panerai, Italy (184), Piaget, Switzerland (123), TUMI Germany (271, 299)